Dedicated to:
Michelle & Tom
June 24, 2023

Written by: Abigail Gartland

I was born six months before my cousin, Jesus.

My story begins with my parents, Zechariah and Elizabeth.

My mom and dad wanted children but did not have any. They grew too old to have children.

One day, the Angel Gabriel, appeared to hem. He told them that they would have a son and name him John.

It was a miracle that my parents had a baby in their old age!

I spent the early years of my life spreading the word of God.

As a part of my mission, I baptized people in the Jordan River.

One day, Jesus asked me to baptize Him.

When I baptized Him, Heaven opened up, and the Holy Spirit appeared as a dove.

As we were all looking up, we heard a voice say, "This is my beloved Son, in whom I am well pleased."

After the baptism of Jesus, I became very well known. King Herod, did not like this and had me arrested.

I was happy to sacrifice for Jesus, who is the Savior of the World.

It is said in the bible that I am the greatest man to have ever lived.

Do you want to be more like me?

You can celebrate my feast day with me on June 24th.

I pray for you every day of your life.

St. John the Baptist, pray for us!

opyright:

part: © PentoolPixie © LimeandKiwiDesigns
ensed purchased: 1/10/2024

About the Author

Abigail Gartland

I love the saints and I love my faith. The idea for sharing the stories of the saints with little ones came when my dear friends were expecting their first baby. I wanted to create something as unique and special as our friendship. Each book is dedicated to very special people and groups who have enriched my faith in different ways. I am blessed to write these stories and appreciate the unending support of my family and friends. When I am not writing, am a middle school teacher. I hope you enjoy these stories. I pray for each and every person who opens one of my books to learn more about the saints.

Abbie

www.ingramcontent.com/pod-product-compliance
Lightning Source LLC
LaVergne TN
LVHW051043070526
838201LV00067B/4900